mel bay presents
Songs of the Jazz Age

Compilation and Editorials by Ian Whitcomb

Edited by Ronny S. Schiff
Chord symbols by Ian Whitcomb

We are grateful to the following companies for permission to use their recordings:
Stomp Off Records - Take Two Records - Audiophile Records-Dick Carty Archives - ITW Records

Special thanks to Tex Wyndham and Dick Zimmerman for lending original sheet music from their collections.

The music on the recording that accompanies the book is played by
Ian Whitcomb and his orchestras with vocals by Ian Whitcomb, except where indicated.

"Prisoner of Love" is sung by Regina Whitcomb, with orchestra conducted by David Raksin.

CD CONTENTS

#	Track
1	Bright Eyes [2:45]
2	Cabaret Girl [2:38]
3	Carolina in the Morning [4:39]
4	Charleston (The Tennessee Tooters) [1:14]
5	Chong [3:01]
6	(I'll See You in) C-U-B-A (Billy Murray) [1:37]
7	Everybody Step (Benny Kreuger's Orchestra) [1:42]
8	A Good Man is Hard to Find (Blue Coal Minstrels) [2:08]
9	I Ain't Got Nobody (Sophie Tucker) [2:32]
10	I Wish I Could Shimmy Like My Sister Kate [3:15]
11	I'm Nobody's Baby (Marion Harris) [3:16]
12	In Hollywood! [2:48]
13	(I Used to Love You But) It's All Over Now [2:20]
14	Just a Girl that Men Forget (Irving Kaufman) [3:00]
15	Limehouse Blues (Paul Whiteman's Orchestra) [1:39]
16	Long Lost Mamma (Daddy Misses You) [4:14]
17	Lovin' Sam (Miss Patricola) [3:08]
18	Margie (Gene Rodemich's Orchestra) [1:19]
19	My Confession [2:18]
20	Prisoner of Love [4:01]
21	Rose of Washington Square (Kentucky Serenaders) [1:25]
22	She Knows It [2:19]
23	The Sheik of Araby (California Ramblers) [3:00]
24	Steppin' Out [2:25]
25	There'll Be Some Changes Made (Marion Harris) [3:04]
26	Who's Sorry Now? [3:07]
27	Wonderful One (Singin' Sam) [4:06]

© 1999 BY MEL BAY PUBLICATIONS, INC., PACIFIC, MO 63069.
ALL RIGHTS RESERVED. INTERNATIONAL COPYRIGHT SECURED. B.M.I. MADE AND PRINTED IN U.S.A.
No part of this publication may be reproduced in whole or in part, or stored in a retrieval system, or transmitted in any form
or by any means, electronic, mechanical, photocopy, recording, or otherwise, without written permission of the publisher.

Visit us on the Web at http://www.melbay.com — E-mail us at email@melbay.com

About the Author

Ian Whitcomb, born in England in 1941, has performed popular songs since childhood. At prep school, he organized a comb-and-tissue paper band to play such current hits as "Answer Me" and "Shrimp Boats"; at boarding school he introduced his version of rock 'n' roll. In his late teens, he discovered ragtime and rhythm & blues. While he was a history major at Trinity College, Dublin, in the early 1960s, he studied, wrote about, and played American pop. By chance, his recording of a novelty song he'd made up, "You Turn Me On," shot him into the American Top Ten in 1965.

As a rock star, Whitcomb toured with the Rolling Stones and the Beach Boys, but his interest in the roots of pop, especially ragtime and Tin Pan Alley, caused him to neglect his teen idol career and to concentrate on researching and performing this largely forgotten music.

The result has been a flow of books, records, documentaries, radio shows, and concerts. He has played everywhere, from the Hollywood Bowl and the Montreux Jazz Festival to shopping malls and private homes. He has contributed, on record and sheet music, his own rags and songs in the grand old Alley tradition. He was even allowed to perform on "The Tonight Show," "Today," and "Tom Snyder." For over a decade, he spread the "word" in Southern California via his radio show on NPR affiliate stations. He lives near the mountains in Altadena, California with his singing wife Regina. Recently, Ian produced the Grammy-award winning CD *Titanic–Music As Heard on the Fateful Voyage* (Rhino Records).

BOOKS BY IAN WHITCOMB

After the Ball: Pop Music from Rag to Rock (1972)
Tin Pan Alley: A Pictorial History (1975)
Lotusland: A Story of Southern California (1979)
Whole Lotta Shakin': A Rock 'n' Roll Scrapbook (1982)
Rock Odyssey: A Chronicle of the Sixties (1983)
Irving Berlin & Ragtime America (1987)
Resident Alien (1990)
The Beckoning Fairground: Notes of a British Exile (1994)
Treasures of Tin Pan Alley (1994)
Vaudeville Favorites (1995)
The Best of Vintage Dance (1996)
Songs of the Ragtime Era (1997)
The Titanic Songbook (1998)
Titanic Tunes–Songs from Steerage (1998)

Contents

INTRODUCTION 5

THE MUSIC

    BRIGHT EYES 37

    CABARET GIRL 129

    CAROLINA IN THE MORNING 82

    CHARLESTON 124

    CHONG 24

    (I'll See You In) C-U-B-A 27

    EVERYBODY STEP 54

    GOOD MAN IS HARD TO FIND, A 20

    I AIN'T GOT NOBODY 14

    I WISH I COULD SHIMMY LIKE MY SISTER KATE 76

    I'M NOBODY'S BABY 59

    IN HOLLYWOOD! 137

    (I Used To Love You But) IT'S ALL OVER NOW 41

    JUST A GIRL THAT MEN FORGET 107

    LIMEHOUSE BLUES 87

    LONG LOST MAMMA (Daddy Misses You) 112

    LOVIN' SAM (The Sheik Of Alabam') 70

    MARGIE 45

    MY CONFESSION 140

    PRISONER OF LOVE 132

    ROSE OF WASHINGTON SQUARE 32

    SHE KNOWS IT 64

    SHEIK OF ARABY, THE 49

    STEPPIN' OUT 102

    THERE'LL BE SOME CHANGES MADE 97

    WHO'S SORRY NOW? 118

    WONDERFUL ONE 93

Introduction

To modern ears, "Jazz Age," meaning the music of the Roaring 'Twenties, is a misnomer. "Jazz" these days refers to music from Duke Ellington to Wynton Marsalis, with a lot of altered chords, atonality, exotic scales, improvisation, and maybe a little rock-fusion, contributing to this original American art form. Jazz means you're cool, hip, and even happening, in a sophisticated way. Jazz certainly isn't to be confused with Dixieland. Nor is jazz to be lumped with pop.

But back in 1917, when the word first appeared in the press, jazz meant a certain sound from a certain band. In January of that year, with the Great War still raging in Europe, The Original Dixieland Jazz Band were about to create a sensation at Reisenweber's, a top night spot in New York. The five boys from New Orleans would introduce a new kind of music – wild and crazy and seemingly free-form. Perfect for a war-weary generation, geared up to expect any mad thing to happen.

The New Orleans boys had picked up the new word while playing a Chicago café the year before. At that time the word was purely oral and nobody knew the correct spelling: was it "jass" or "jasz" or "jazz"? Did it originate with "Jasbo Brown," a legendary black street performer, or was the word a corruption of the French "jaser," meaning "to chatter"? In 1833 Henry Palmerston, British Prime Minister, wrote in a letter about a man "jazzing and telling stories". So perhaps the original meaning of the word concerned spinning a yarn or improvising — telling tall stories in order to keep your listener's attention. Some said that it was simply a slang expression for the sexual act.

However, the New Orleans boys would have none of this. They maintained that one night, while tooting their lively dance music in the Chicago café, an inebriated customer demanded they "jazz it up." This, roughly speaking, meant "screw it up," or, more musically, to have some fun with the tune by cutting loose, by improvising, by exaggerating the song in a grotesque manner. To hell with the printed music – these boys couldn't read anyway! That was the point – anarchy.

In fact, the members of The Original Dixieland Jazz Band were quite conservative musicians ringing only slight changes on a kind of syncopated musical style that had been developing slowly in underground America, far from conservatories and even Tin Pan Alley. The style, hot and gingerly played in a tight contrapuntal ensemble, had specifically been nurtured in multicultural New Orleans. The basis was *ragtime*. Up in New York, performing at the trendy night spot, the Dixie band sounded like a cut-down military band gone crazy, when all they were playing was a rootsy, folksy kind of controlled chaos.

Billed as "Untuneful Harmonists Playing Peppery Melodies" and "The Sensational Amusement Novelty of 1917," they were soon the talk of the town and "Jazz" became the latest buzzword. Their first record on Victor was released that year and sold over a million copies – the first real million seller. The next year, 1919, they became the highest paid dance band in the nation. Thus: jazz meant best-selling pop music and also music for dancing. The music business wanted a part of the action…

Dance band leaders and vaudeville stars quickly took notes on the "new music," with its accompanying post-war "could care less" attitude and appropriate defiant posturing for the newspaper photographers. The Original Dixieland Jazz Band musicians were pictured taming wild beasts in the zoo with jazz; their leader boasted: "We are the assassinators of syncopation." Ted Lewis and Jimmy Durante formed jazz bands. Sophie Tucker, casting aside her cloak of ragtime, was now billed as "The Queen of Jazz." The straight house orchestras of the nightclub and hotel business cut their numbers down to a few musicians, with the emphasis on noise and nuttiness. Drums, with plenty of cowbells, woodblocks and fly swatters, became the main attraction. Then, around 1919, came the smooth and sometimes wailing sound of the saxophone-based Art Hickman Dance Band from San Francisco. Tight and tasty, well-rehearsed and reading from arrangements. The jazz band tamed at last!

Finally, by 1921, Paul Whiteman's band (another West Coast ensemble) established the brisk foxtrot style of the 1920s dance/jazz band, dominating the field via million-seller records and a million dollar corporation, complete with press agents and bookers. Whiteman was crowned "King of Jazz" by the press.

More accurately, he was King of the Jazz Age. F. Scott Fitzgerald's clever title included flaming youth and flappers, vamps and sheiks, red-hot mamas, speakeasies and hip flasks, collegiate capers – the age-old rebellion of youth versus age in the new costume of short skirts and Oxford "bags" (trousers), and a contemporary attitude of complete release from the intense moral crusade of the recent Great War. People, said Scott Fitzgerald, had been too long at "moral attention" and so he and his wife, Zelda advocated an endless round of parties. His idea of heaven was to throw "a stupendous house party that went on for days and days…with a medical staff in attendance and the biggest jazz orchestras in the city."

So, for a few years, the American dance band business supplied exciting, peppy and jumpy notes and rhythms. Arrangements were full of nifty syncopated riffs and odd

"Chinesey" chords (borrowed in 1924 by George Gershwin for his "Rhapsody in Blue"). A new kind of singer emerged, blowing hard and blue notes. Mostly they were women—blues mamas with complaints ("A Good Man Is Hard to Find") and warnings to unfaithful lovers ("There'll Be Some Changes Made"). African-American writers were, for a short while, again having their say in popular music. Their songs, such as the above, were, for the most part, sung in vaudeville, on record and radio by white women singers – liberated ladies who could vamp men as sexual prey, who saw men as suckers.

This high-energy jazz age couldn't last. After Paul Whiteman made "a lady out of jazz" by turning it "symphonic" at his historic Aeolian Hall concert in 1924 (in which "Rhapsody in Blue" was introduced, and in which The Original Dixieland Jazz Band was travestied as an example of the crudeness of early jazz), the dance band business turned the feisty little jazz bands into well-drilled regiments of tuxedoed pros, chugging relentlessly into the 'thirties where there would be a pit-stop for streamlining so that there could emerge, gleaming and multi-tiered, the Big Bands of the Swing Age. But that's a later story.

Meanwhile, what of the denizens of Tin Pan Alley, the creators of hits in sheet music form, the original begetters of pop? As usual, as when ragtime had first appeared and ruffled their placid world of ballads and minstrelsy, they watched and noted and synthesized. They found ways to notate and stylize the hot licks and blue-note crushes of jazz; they found lyric expression for the new breed of jazz babies and fresh college boys. They wrote of Dapper Dan and Lovin' Sam and Girls That Men Forget. The new hedonism was just an advance on the old ragtime shouters.

The Alleymen also realized that the burgeoning dance band business needed a different kind of song: slicker, simpler, with short verses and an instantly catchy chorus, and melody lines with gaps where a clever arranger could insert some current jazzy riffs. The writers also set out to standardize the pop song down to a neat 32 bars: a main strain, then a short different tune (called the "bridge" or "release"), and finally back to the main strain. A perfect commercial package, good for dance floors, and radio broadcasts. *Radio*—soon to become the major platform for launching a song trend, to repeat songs by the hour, gobbling them up so fast that the publishers were forced into manufacturing this homogenized song product.

However, we are talking here about the late 'twenties. In the early Jazz Age, when nobody knew the rules, there was still room for some quirkiness. There was still time for topical event songs (an old tradition), for a ragtimey feeling, for numbers that didn't necessarily have a bridge or the strict 32 bars. All in all, this period (circa 1918-1924) is a fascinating transition time between the end of ragtime (and the last vestiges of nineteenth century minstrelsy) and the establishment of a modern music industry embracing fast-moving technologies such as radio, records, and talking pictures, in order to service them with a slick factory-made product. The New York-based music business (later to link with Los Angeles in the 1940s) was to be the dictator, control-

ling pop music until the great rebellion of rock 'n' roll. And, musically, this rock 'n' roll of the middle 'fifties bore a strong resemblance to ragtime: a similar rhythm and cold shower liveliness; an evangelical excitement as opposed to a world-weary cynicism.

Let us examine our collection of early Jazz Age songs to see how old Tin Pan Alley song models and stock characters survived by being refashioned for the new age. In truth, the "new age" only at first applied to Big City, sophisticated America, because the majority of the nation lived in small towns and rural communities where the old values and the old certainties still held sway. Seasons change, but they always come around again. Small town America's world was cyclical and circular, not jazz age progressive. Even so, through newspapers and, more importantly, radio, the latest goings-on slowly insinuated themselves into Average American life: respectable ordinary folk, especially their young ones, became aware of petting parties, taped-down breasts, hooch in the hip flask, sheiks and shebas in topless Fords, and the teachings of Freud. Sex reared its ugly head and couldn't stop talking. Everybody was discussing it; good girls were doing it. There was a sharp decline in prostitution.

And yet, just as in the rocking 'fifties, a good many of the best-selling songs were romantic ballads, especially waltzes. Perhaps with the frantic pace of a life with telephones, automobiles, and airplanes, people needed time out for romantic, dreamy music, leading to some sensible moonlight cuddling. Moonlight hadn't changed, nor had the roses. So there were the beautiful wrenching harmonies, and almost Victorian sentiments of the waltz, "Wonderful One." The tune was by the great film director Marshall Neilan, who first hummed it to Gloria Swanson in Paris. Theodora Morse, wife of hit songwriter Theodore Morse ("M-O-T-H-E-R," and others) set Neilan's tune to words under her pseudonym of "Dorothy Terriss"; a little polishing was done by, of all people, "The King of Jazz" himself, Paul Whiteman, assisted by his longtime arranger, Ferdie Grofé. Another hit waltz, and a cautionary tale warning of the pitfalls of leading the jazz baby life, was "Just a Girl That Men Forget." Al Dubin, long before his partnership with Harry Warren and the stream of smart sophisticated 1930s musicals they worked on together, contributed the pulpit-pounding lyric: the aging flapper is only a toy to enjoy for awhile, and when her old-fashioned sister is getting married she'll be stuck outside the church, abandoned.

In "Who's Sorry Now?" revenge is proved to be sweet. Most of us know this evergreen as a fast number, a jazz classic. However, it too was originally a waltz – a "valse moderato," to be exact. Kalmar and Ruby, the lyricists, were later to be famous for snappy stuff like "Three Little Words," and for their Marx Brothers material. Composer Ted Snyder, an Alley veteran, had hired the kid Irving Berlin as a staff writer with the

Snyder Publishing Company back in 1908. One of the results was "Alexander's Ragtime Band" in 1911. In Snyder's Jazz Age waltz, we must note the haunting harmonies of the chorus, those sad sevenths – it would seem that Liszt's "Leibestraum" was the first number to present us with such a chord sequence; composers have used it many times since. After the second waltz chorus, we are offered a foxtrot version, perfect for neophyte jazzers with its insistent four-four beat. The Alleymen were taking no chances, they were covering all bases.

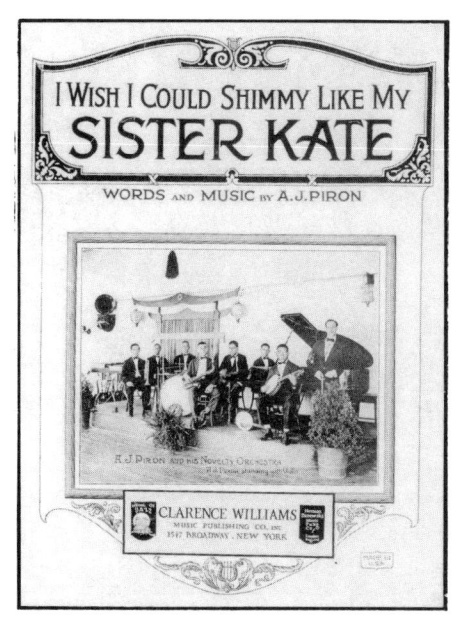

Jazz babies, armed with the vote and an attitude, were celebrated in "I Wish I Could Shimmy Like My Sister Kate." To be precise, it's a *problem* that's described here: Kate is attracting all the boys in the neighborhood with some sinuous, shiver-shaking of her hips – the shimmy was a sexy dance movement made famous on stage by Gilda Gray and Mae West. Poor "Rose of Washington Square," as portrayed by Fanny Brice in *The Zeigfeld Midnight Frolic*, is a slave to basement painters sporting long hair and secondhand clothes, offering her Roman nose as artistic inspiration to frequenters of "Bohemian Honky Tonks" in Greenwich Village, precursors of 1950s Beatniks and 1960s Hippies. The tune is a lovely one, and the song is the work of veteran Alleymen.

That it could be a tough life as a 1920s female hedonist is shown in "I'm Nobody's Baby," in which a blissful childhood of being knee-bounced is compared to the lonely, desperate city life of the jazz age. The girl is offering herself to anybody, to everybody. Benny Davis, one of the writers, had his first hit in the recent war ("Goodbye Broadway, Hello France") and his last one in the early 1960s, when Connie Francis went to the top of the charts with "Don't Break the Heart That Loves You." In between, there was "Baby Face." Milton Ager, another contributor and the man who taught George Gershwin the art of arranging, was to have a nice run of hits when he collaborated with Jack Yellen ("Happy Days Are Here Again," "Ain't She Sweet," and more – our offering here, "Lovin' Sam").

The misery blues songs seem to have been started with "I Ain't Got Nobody," a piquant slice of self-pity that first appeared with its famous title in 1916. There's an earlier version, published the year before, called "I Ain't Go Nobody Much." Rather wry humor, suggesting that the girl has a few standby casual lovers, but no real love of her own. It appears that the song started life in 1914 as an unpublished manuscript by Charles Warfield and David Young. Warfield was a quite well-known St. Louis ragtime composer and pianist. Somehow, possibly due to music business machinations, the song ends up credited to two different writers, Spencer Williams and Roger Graham. Both, incidentally, were in the music publishing game. The tune, with its falling chorus chords, positively drips with tears.

The males made their position reasonably clear when talking about the latest hot mamas: "She Knows It" describes, in broad vaudeville strokes, a girl whose "middle name's conceit," but "one minute with her alone and she can break up your home – and she knows it." When at last the flapper settles down to marriage, battle is joined in the kitchen: "Steppin' Out" is the action taken by a husband battered by "dishes and rolling pins, pots and pans." He informs wifey that he can be found night and day in "any swell café." The new tough guy's philosophy was undone a few years later by the coming of those caressers of the microphone— the crooners. Men became gentlemen again. In my recorded version I mis-read "tear" as in weeping rather than as in the crazed spree meant by the writers of this song. Yet I prefer my mistake: a poetic vision is summoned up.

Interest in the exotic, an old Alley subject, did not disappear with the Jazz Age. "Chong," a Chinese drummer, is tired of his native music where singers "cry way up high, singee, sungay, mungay." No, he prefers American ragtime and he'll even sail to Hong Kong and bring back his bride so that she can dance the shimmy and sing the latest Yankee music, be it ragtime or jazz. It's all-American and therefore exciting and novel.

In reverse, "The Sheik of Araby," inspired by the hit novel (and later the movie), *The Sheik*, tells of a dusky lover boy (sleek and sallow and probably Rudolph Valentino) announcing in the chorus that he intends to creep into a lady's tent. And then what? Middle America might well shudder. The tune, with its insistent use of the sixth, is by our old Alleyman, Ted Snyder.

From England, of all places, came "Limehouse Blues," introduced to Americans in the Broadway show, *Charlot's Revue*. Who'd have guessed that British writers could create such a bluesy chord sequence? And such an eerie, exotic atmosphere? Those who knew London understood that Limehouse was where the Chinese lived, not far from where Jack the Ripper had operated.

Dixie was not about to be upstaged by faraway foreign places. The glories of the South were celebrated in "Carolina In the Morning," and who could resist the idea of "strolling with my girlie where the day is pearly early in the morning"? Especially when the tune rocks catchily from third to tonic and back again, like a see-saw. Walter Donaldson, the composer, is supposed to have gotten this little tune from a musical toy belonging to the child of his lyricist, Gus Kahn. The same toy inspired "My Buddy." The trick of Donaldson's in "Carolina" was to lay a descending line and some changing chords under the repetitive melody in order to avoid overdoing the see-saw effect and thus creating monotony. Thomas Edison, who ran his record label with a hands-on policy, would have nothing to do with "Carolina." Boasting that he could spot a potential hit by merely having its tune hummed at him, he told his scout to forget about the Donaldson melody. Without the harmony, the number just doesn't work. Clever Alleymen knew all about the rich candy of harmony.

Especially in the know was Irving Berlin, the Alley King, who was now discarding the word "ragtime" for "jazz." In "Alexander's Ragtime Band" he had encouraged the world to come on and hear the latest craze of ragtime. In the jazz age, in "Everybody Step", he was issuing the same invitation to join in the fun, only now it's all about strutting to a syncopated four-four jazz beat. And what a cunningly syncopated rhythm! Only Berlin could have concocted those pushy, nervy phrases – like New Yorkers rushing to do something fast, anything at all. To return to the harmony point: the melody jerks along in a major mode and then suddenly, on the words "Come, come don't hesitate," goes minor and modal before jumping back into the light of a western day. Very tasty indeed – like a sweet and sour sauce. In "I'll See You in C-U-B-A," he plays the same trick, darting from minor to major and back in the verse, and then plunging us into a very romantic interval at the start of the chorus – an interval used to soaring effect decades earlier by Saint-Saëns in his famous aria from *Samson and Delilah*. Berlin's song is no simple travel poster: he's commenting on Prohibition, pointing out that in Cuba "wine is flowing" and thus "all is happy." All was not happy on Broadway as a result of the alcohol ban: smart restaurants, elegant bars and nightclubs took a dive and were replaced, at street level, by cheap chop suey joints, radio stores and penny arcades. "Forty-Second Street" was in the making.

Finally we must return to the main stage – to the *jazz dance*.

The "Charleston" is eternally identified with the Roaring 'Twenties. This odd pigeon-toed step is rather ugly and ungainly when one considers it soberly, but it became, and still remains, the archetypal jazz age movement, all frenzy and jerkiness, perhaps even dysfunctional. Quite intoxicating: the grand entrance you make into a non-stop party. At the time, the dance steps appeared very un-European, most indecorous. Indeed, they had originated in ancient Africa and been carried across to America where they had lain underground until the ragtime dance craze of 1912 to 1917 pulled them up into the open. James P. Johnson, the black composer and pianist who pioneered jazz "stride" piano, composed the music to the song, "Charleston," while Cecil Mack, whose real name was Cecil McPherson, wrote the words. The number, together with their opposing ballad, a sweet and sentimental song called "Old Fashioned Love," was introduced in the Broadway show, *Runnin' Wild* in 1923.

In the song, the setting is the standard sunny South where everything in the line of ragtime and jazz is supposed to have started. In such songs, the listener is urged to be in fashion or else – the old buck-and-wing, says the lyrics is now a "back number" so you must get "religion in your feet" because "every step you do leads to something new." "New" – the all-American passion. Interesting, then, that the harmony of the chorus is so Victorian, much of it following the sequence from Liszt that we noted in "Who's Sorry Now?"

The characteristic Charleston rhythm trick is very zesty and enticing, seeming to buck the usual beat, bouncing in like an uninvited but terribly exciting party guest. However, after a marathon of Charlestoning, you'd need the respite of a balmy waltz and, as we've seen, there was no lack of waltzes in the Jazz Age. James P. Johnson, the jazz master, wrote some excellent ones ("Eccentricity" is an example).

Notice that the tablature that was developed for the ukulele became a regular part of pop sheet music. A little later, we were to be provided with chord symbols for guitarists (and for piano players who aren't so sharp at sight reading and need an aid). The uke diagrams were added in response to the enormous popularity of this little instrument, with its pleasing plunk, and easy strumming and chording. It had first appeared in America via Hawaiian acts in vaudeville around 1916. Soon, young lovers discovered the simplicity of producing music on the uke and the advantages, especially when out-of-doors on a blanket or in a canoe, of wooing one's partner with this portable love machine.

The Twenties marked the beginning of the end of the glorious and unrivaled reign of Tin Pan Alley – of sheet music as the boss of pop. Radio, records, and finally talking pictures were to take away the Alley's crown. The public would slowly give up the making of music through the study of piano scores and would take up the passivity produced by the new electronic technologies of entertainment.

Yet today, despite the profusion of electronic push-button entertainment, some of us are becoming "retro" in the best sense of the word – returning to do-it-yourself music-making, whether it be hammered dulcimer or hurdy-gurdy. The ukulele has made a come-back – there's a magnificently-produced book available containing all you need to know about the instrument and its history* – piano sales are up. Ragtime and classic jazz festivals thrive around America and are even to be found as far away as Hungary. I know because it's at these festivals that I spend blissful hours in safe surroundings performing the old songs to the accompaniment of my ukulele. I perform the music not for reasons of nostalgia – I never knew the jazz age – but because my heart responds to its sentiments and sounds. I even create my own songs in the classic form: "Cabaret Girl" from my musical *Lotusland*, set in the 1920s, and "Prisoner of Love" from a *Roaring Twenties* revue at the Thunderbird Hotel, Las Vegas, in the 1970s. "In Hollywood," although a jaunty jazz age tune, was written as a sardonic comment on the sleaziness of Hollywood in the 1970s. However, Hollywood is getting a face-lift and will be glorious once more. So we are taking care of our past at last, and making sure it fits snugly into the cultural and convenient demands of the present. Speaking of the present, my final offering is "My Confession," a song of praise and thanks to my wife Regina, who fills so many roles on my behalf that she sounds like a million Alley songs rolled into one. She is my everything and my everybody and so that's why I wrote the song. It's not *correct* but I like it.

The Ukulele – A Visual History, by Jim Beloff. Miller Freeman Books, San Francisco, 1997. Also, check out *Legends of Ukulele* (Rhino Records CD R275278) for recordings by "Ukulele Ike", Tiny Tim, and me. And watch out for my next Mel Bay Songbook/CD called *Ukulele Heaven: The Golden Age of the Ukulele*.

I AIN'T GOT NOBODY MUCH

Words by
ROGER GRAHAM.

Music by
SPENCER WILLIAMS.

There's a say-ing go-ing 'round, And I be-gin to think it's true,___ It's aw-ful hard to love some-one When
If I on-ly had some-one That I could on-ly call my own,___ For I would mar-ry them at once And

International Copyright Secured.

Copyright MCMXVI by Craig & Company,
Copyright transferred, MCMXVI, to Frank K. Root & Co.

All Rights Reserved.

CHONG
(He Come From Hong Kong)

Words and Music by
HAROLD WEEKS
Writer of "Hindustan"

Moderato

Till Voice

Lit-tle Al-lee Fo Chong played all day in an or-i-en-tal way, — In a
Lit-tle Al-lee Fo Chong sailed a-way on the lin-er "Sak-o-shay," — For his

swell Chin-ese Ca-fé, — But Al-lee loved his rag the same as you, — And ev-'ry evening when his
home port far a-way, — He said, "When I come back I bring-ee bride, — You see a Chi-na maid-en

work was thru, — Al-lee layed his Tom Tom down, Pret-ty soon you hear this sound:
by my side, — Al-lee know she wait for he, Ev-'ry day so pa-tient-ly."

CHORUS

"Chong, ———— he come from Hong Kong ———— where Chin-ee-man play all-ee

Also published for Male or Mixed Voices 15¢ Band or Orchestra 25¢
Copyright MCMXIX by LEO. FEIST, Inc. Feist Bldg., N.Y.
International Copyright Secured and Reserved
London — Herman Darewski Mus. Pub. Co.

OPERATIC EDITION
I'LL SEE YOU IN
C-U-B-A
by IRVING BERLIN
As featured in the Greenwich Village Follies
by "The JAZZ KING" TED LEWIS
Price 60¢
Irving Berlin, Inc.
Music Publishers
1587 Broadway
New York

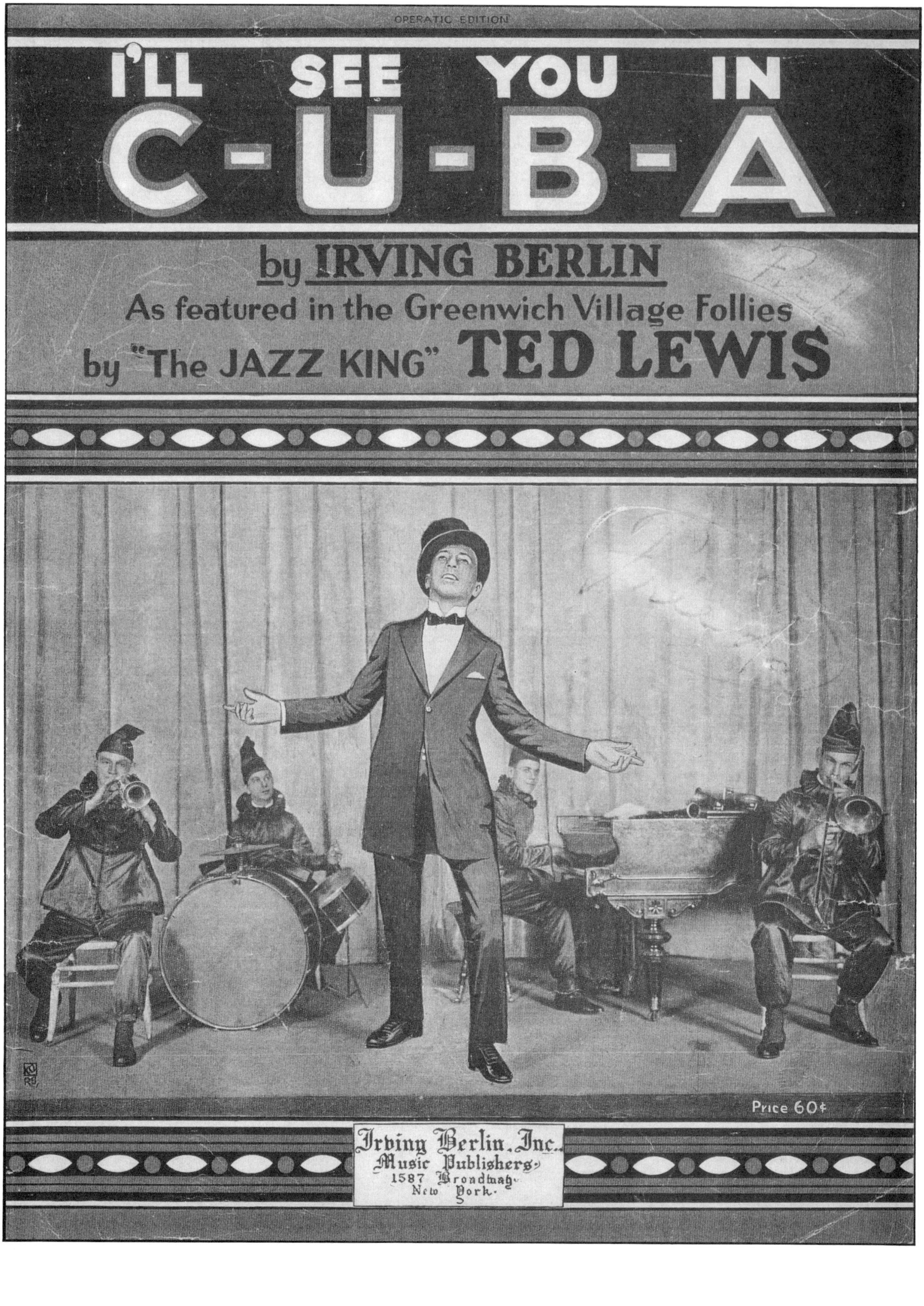

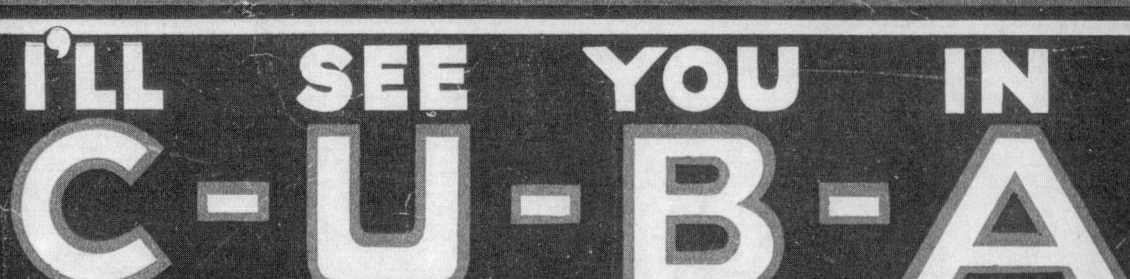

I Used To Love You But It's All Over Now

Lyrics by
LEW BROWN

Melody by
ALBERT VON TILZER

Marcia moderato *(not too fast)*

Moderato
Till ready

I used to bless the day I first met you
I nev-er would be-lieve the things I'd hear
I planned so man-y things for just us two — But now its plain to
Be-cause I al-ways thought you were sin-cere — But now I find I'm
see — that you have nev-er cared for me
wrong — for you've been flirt-ing right a - long
You can't de-ny you fooled me
You will ad-mit I act-ed

Copyright MCMXX by Broadway Music Corporation, 145 W. 45th St., N.Y.
All Rights Reserved   British Copyright Secured   Will Von Tilzer, Pres.   International Copyright Secured
The Publisher reserves the right to the use of this Copyrighted work upon the parts of Instruments serving to reproduce it Mechanically

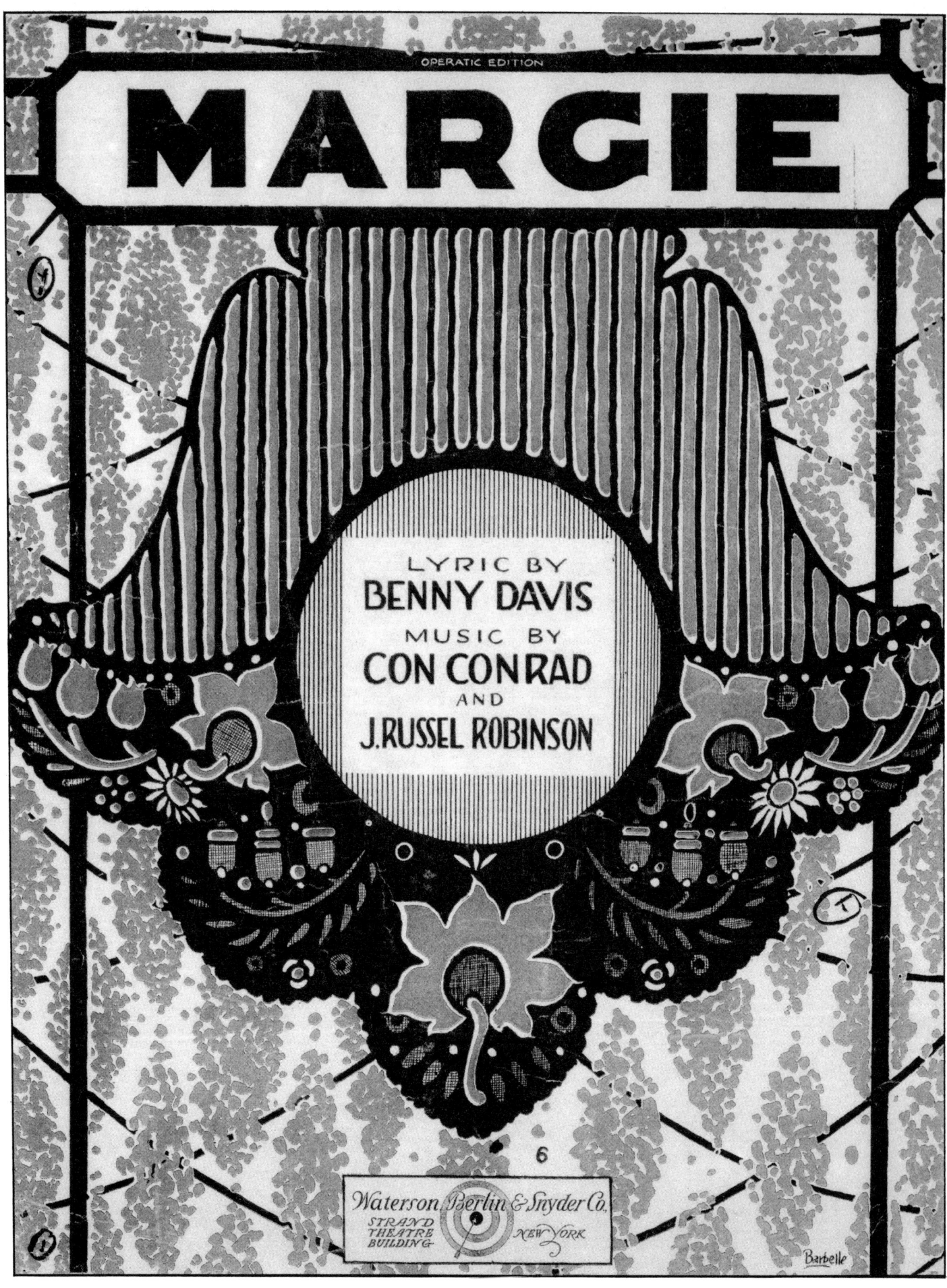

MARGIE

Lyric by
BENNY DAVIS

Music by
CON CONRAD and
J. RUSSEL ROBINSON

You can talk a-bout your love af-fairs, Here's one I must tell to you; All night long they sit up-
You can pic-ture me most ev-'ry night, I can't wait un-til they start; Ev-'ry thing he says just

Copyright MCMXX by Waterson, Berlin & Snyder Co.
Copyright Canada MCMXX by Waterson, Berlin & Snyder Co.
International Copyright Secured

The Sheik
of Araby

Words by
HARRY B. SMITH
& FRANCIS WHEELER

Music by
TED SNYDER

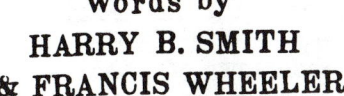

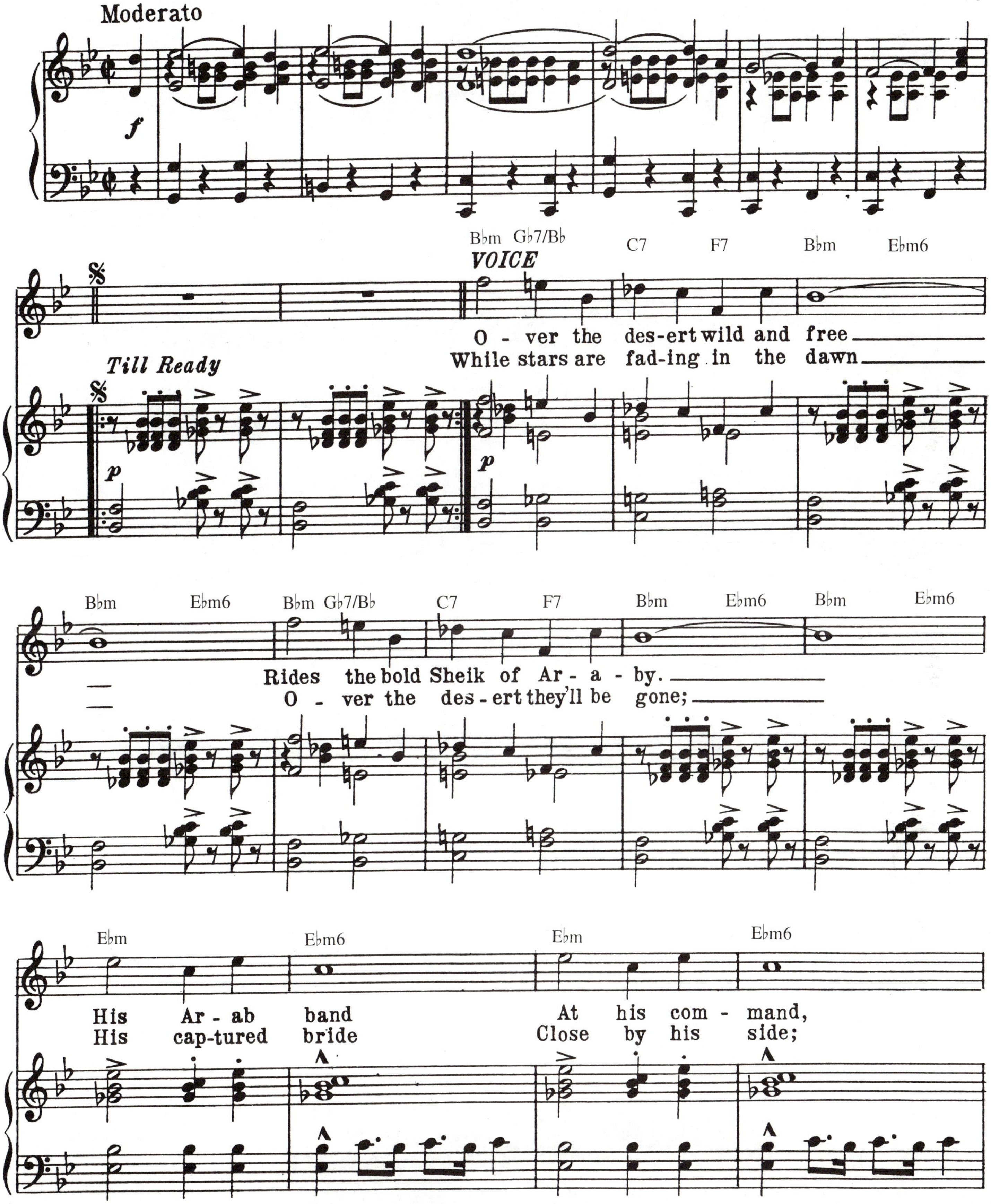

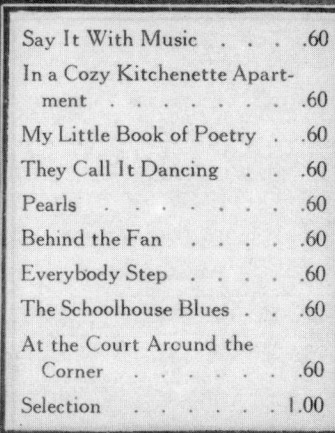

She Knows It

By JACK STERN and
CLARENCE J. MARKS

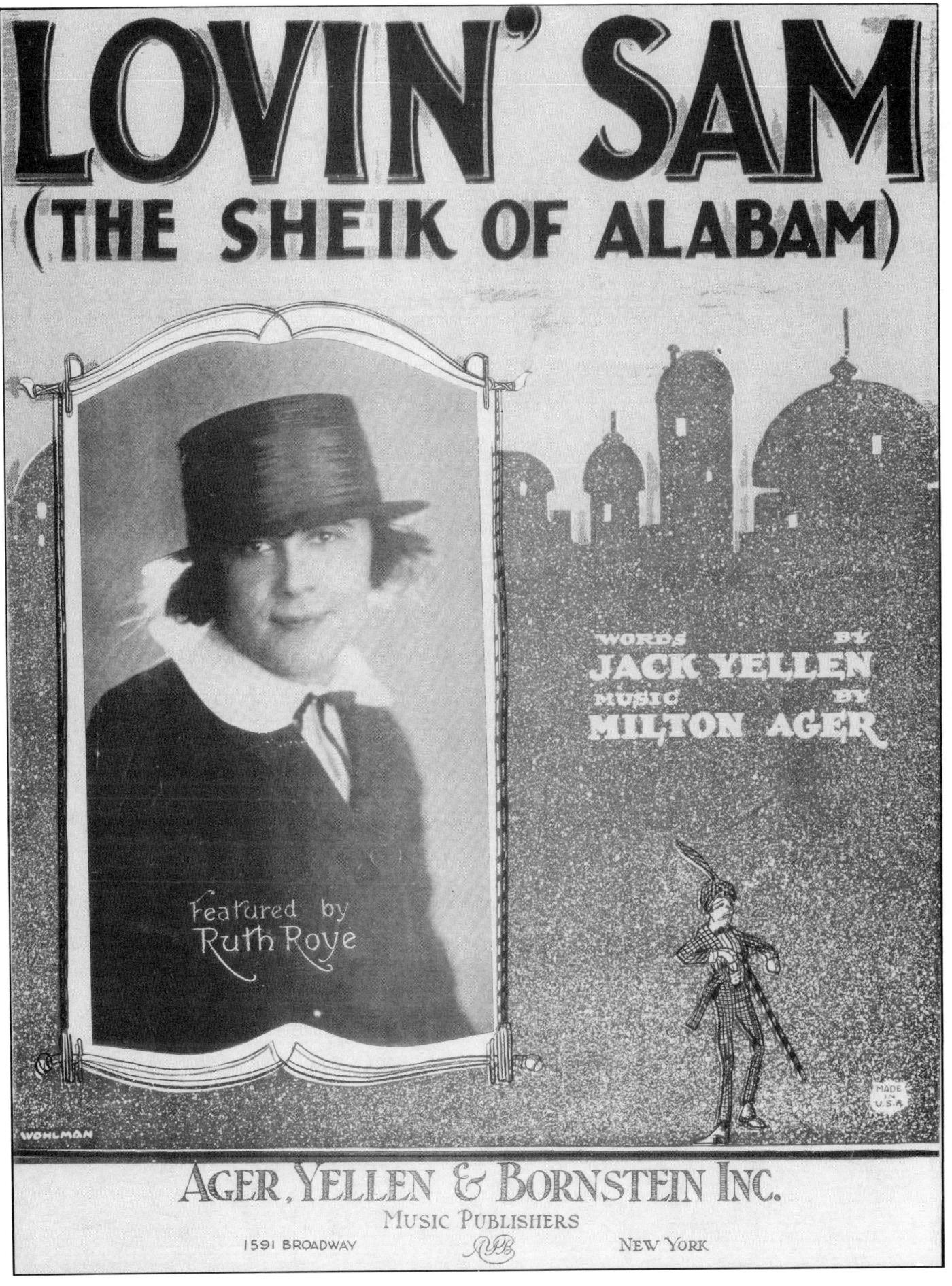

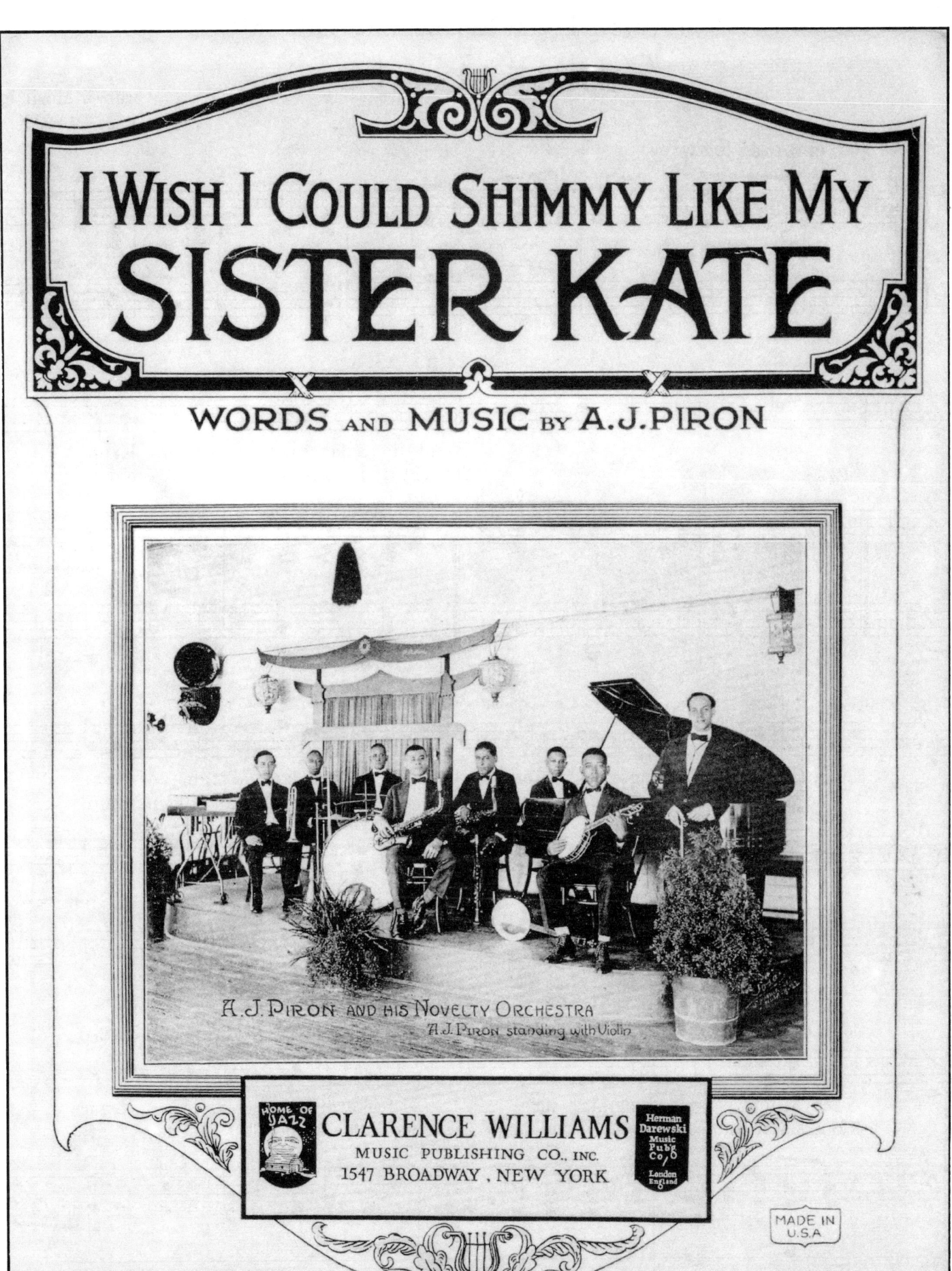

CAROLINA IN THE MORNING
SONG

Lyric by
GUS KAHN

Music by
WALTER DONALDSON

Wish-ing is good-time wast-ed Still it's a hab-it they say
Dream-ing was meant for night-time I live in dreams all the day

Wish-ing for sweets I've tast-ed That's all I do — all day
I know it's not the right time But still I dream a-way

Copyright MCMXXII by JEROME H. REMICK & Co., New York & Detroit
Copyright, Canada, MCMXXII by Jerome H. Remick & Co.
Propiedad para la Republica Mexicana de Jerome H. Remick & Co., New York y Detroit. Depositada conforme a la ley
Performing Rights Reserved

MADE IN U.S.A.

Limehouse Blues

Words by
DOUGLAS FURBER

Music by
PHILIP BRAHAM

Copyright MCMXXII by Ascherberg, Hopwood & Crew, Ltd.

ALL RIGHTS RESERVED
Including Public Performance for Profit

Also Published in A flat

To Julie

Wonderful One

WALTZ SONG

Words by
DOROTHY TERRISS
Author of —"Three O'Clock in the Morning" etc.

Music by
PAUL WHITEMAN and
FERDIE GROFÉ
Adapted from a Theme by
MARSHALL NIELAN

5244-3

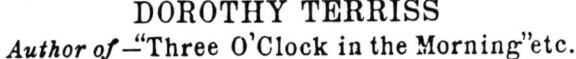

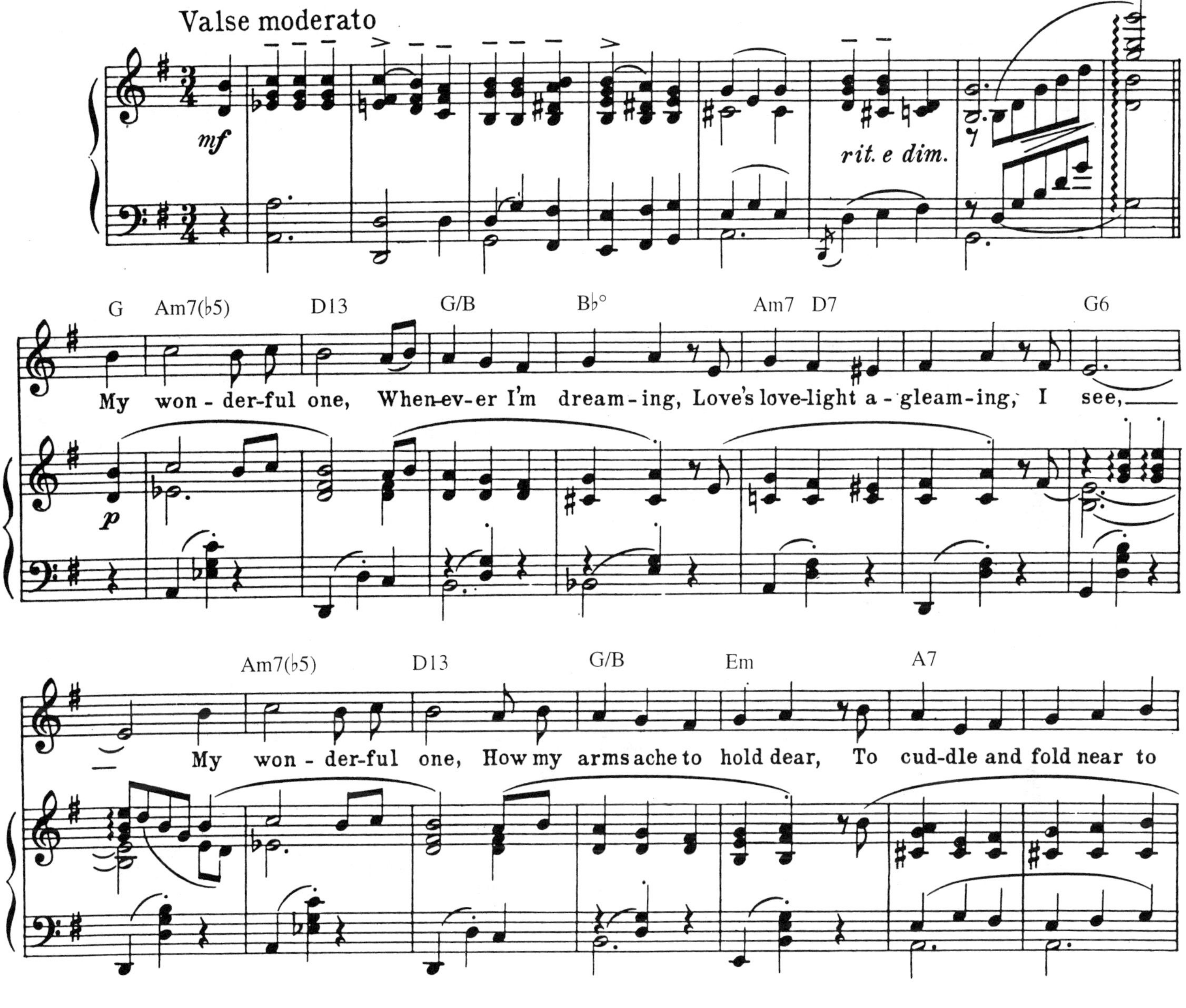

There'll Be Some Changes Made

Lyric by
BILLY HIGGINS

Music by
W. BENTON OVERSTREET

Copyright MCMXXIII by Edw. B. Marks Music Co.
British Copyright Secured
English Theatre and Music Hall rights strictly reserved

Made in U.S.A.

ADDITIONAL CHORUSES
There'll Be Some Changes Made

By WILSON & RINGLE

1. There's a change in your manner
   And a change in your way
   There was time once when you was O. K.
   You once said you saved ev'ry kiss for my sake
   Now you're giving all the girls an even break
   I'm gonna send out invitations to the men I know
   Cause you're gettin' colder than an Eskimo
   I must have my lovin' or I'll fade away
   There'll be some changes made to-day
   There'll be some changes made.

2. For there's a change in your manner
   There's a change in your style
   And here of late you never wear a smile
   You don't seem to act like a real lover should
   You can't thrill your mamma if you're made of wood
   I gotta have a man who loves me like a real live Sheik
   With a tasty kiss that lingers for a week
   I'm not over sixty so it's time to say
   There'll be some changes made to-day
   There'll be some changes made.

3. For there's a change in your squeezin'
   There's a change in your kiss
   It used to have a kick that I now miss
   You'd set me on fire when you used to tease
   Now each time you call I just sit there and freeze
   You had a way of making love that made a hit with me
   One time you could thrill me but it's plain to see
   You're not so ambitious as you used to be
   There'll be some changes made by me
   There'll be some changes made.

4. There's a change in the weather
   There's a change in the sea
   From now on there'll be a change in me
   I'm tired of working all of my life
   I'm gonna grab a rich husband and be his wife
   I'm going to ride around in a big limousine
   Wear fancy clothes and put on plenty of steam
   No more tired puppies, will I treat you mean
   There'll be some changes made to-day
   There'll be some changes made.

5. For there's a change in your manner
   There's a change in your smile
   From now on you can't be worth my while
   I'm right here to tell you with you I'm thru
   Your brand of lovin' will never do
   I'm gettin' tired of eating just butter and bread
   I could enjoy a few pork chops instead
   You know variety is the spice of life they say
   There'll be some changes made to-day (I'll get mine)
   There'll be some changes made.

Copyright assigned MCMXXXII to Edward B. Marks Music Corporation
Copyright MCMXXIV by Edward B. Marks Music Co.

STEPPIN' OUT

SONG

Lyric & Music By
John S. Howard
and
Con Conrad

As Sung by
Van and Schenck

JEROME H. REMICK & CO.

STEPPIN' OUT

SONG

By JOHN S. HOWARD
& CON CONRAD

Just A Girl That Men Forget

Waltz Ballad

By AL DUBIN, FRED RATH and JOE GARREN

Copyright MCMXXIII by Jack Mills Inc. 152 W. 45th St. New York
International Copyright Secured and Reserved
London, England - The Lawrence Wright Music Co. Denmark St., Charing Cross Road

LONG LOST MAMMA
DADDY MISSES YOU.

FOX-TROT BALLAD.

Words and Music by
HARRY WOODS.

Folks a-gree, Sammy Lee Is the bluest man in town,
I've heard blues, Real blue blues, But no bluer blues I say,

Always weepin', ne-ver sleepin', Since his Mamma threw him down; And
For-sa-ken blues, heart ach-in' blues, That just tear your heart a-way; So

Copyright 1923 by M. Witmark & Sons.   For the United Kingdom & British Dominions, excepting Canada & Australasia, B. Feldman & Co., Sole Agents for M. Witmark & Sons.   All rights reserved.

Long lost Mamma.

Long lost Mamma.

Ian's Re-Creations

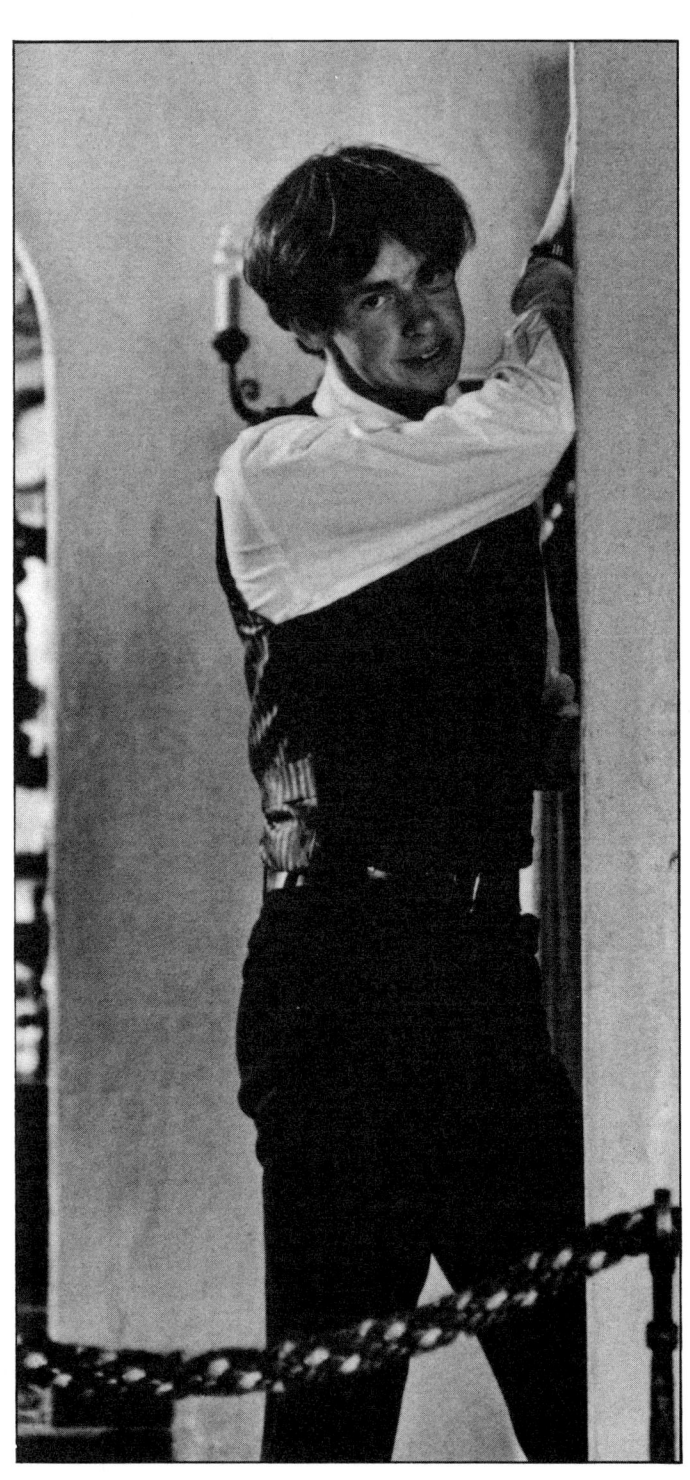

CABARET GIRL

❖

PRISONER OF LOVE

❖

IN HOLLYWOOD!

❖

MY CONFESSION

Cabaret Girl

(From the musical-comedy "Lotusland")

Words & Music by
IAN WHITCOMB
Arranged by David Pinto

Cab - a - ret girl lost in the whirl,

big cit - y blues brought you down.

Once you were bright, light - ing the night,

© 1991 Ian Whitcomb Songs, Box 451, Altadena, California 91003

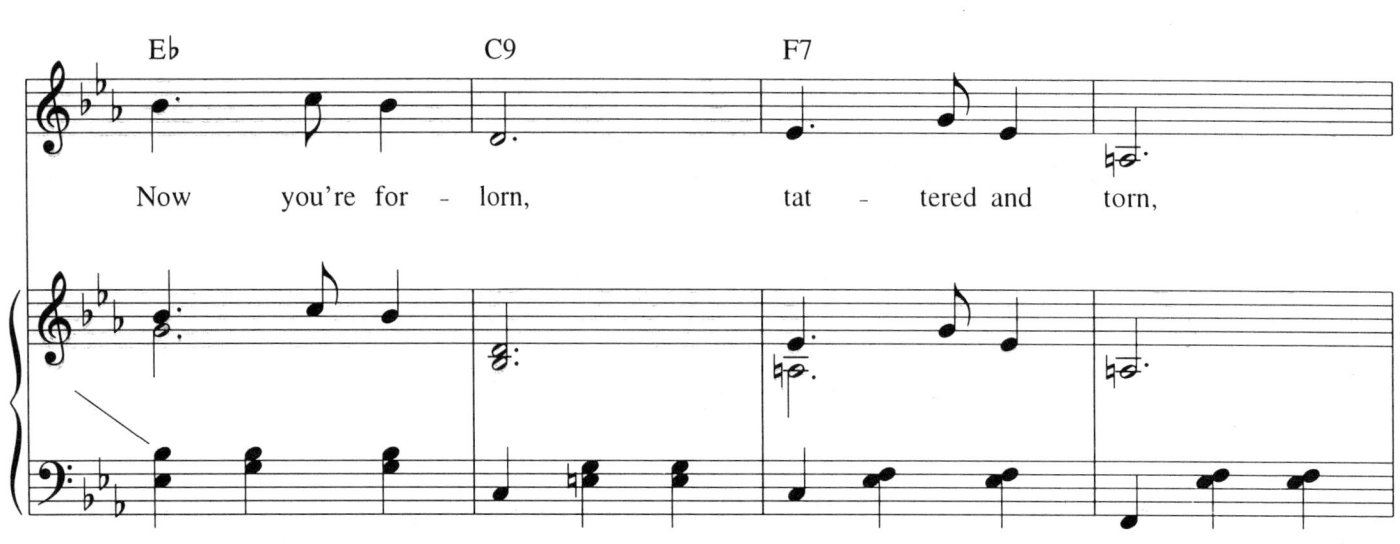
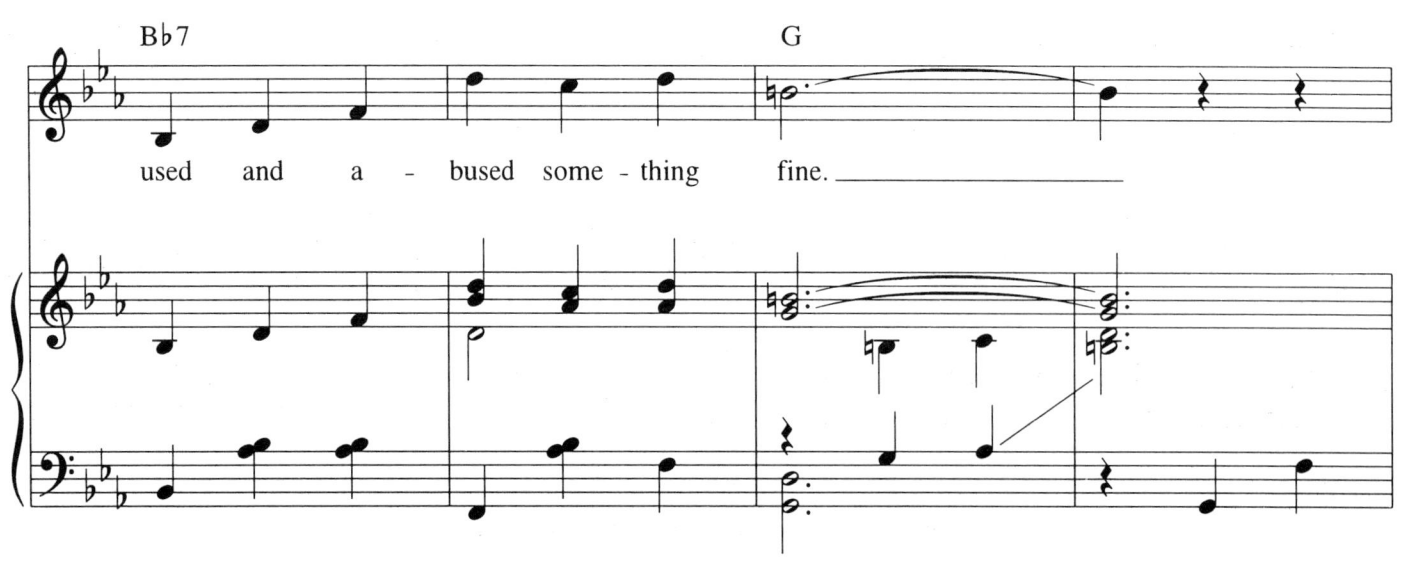

130

Prisoner of Love
(From the musical-comedy "Lotusland")

Words & Music
IAN WHITCOMB
Arranged by David Pinto

© 1975 Ian Whitcomb Songs, Box 451, Altadena, California 91003

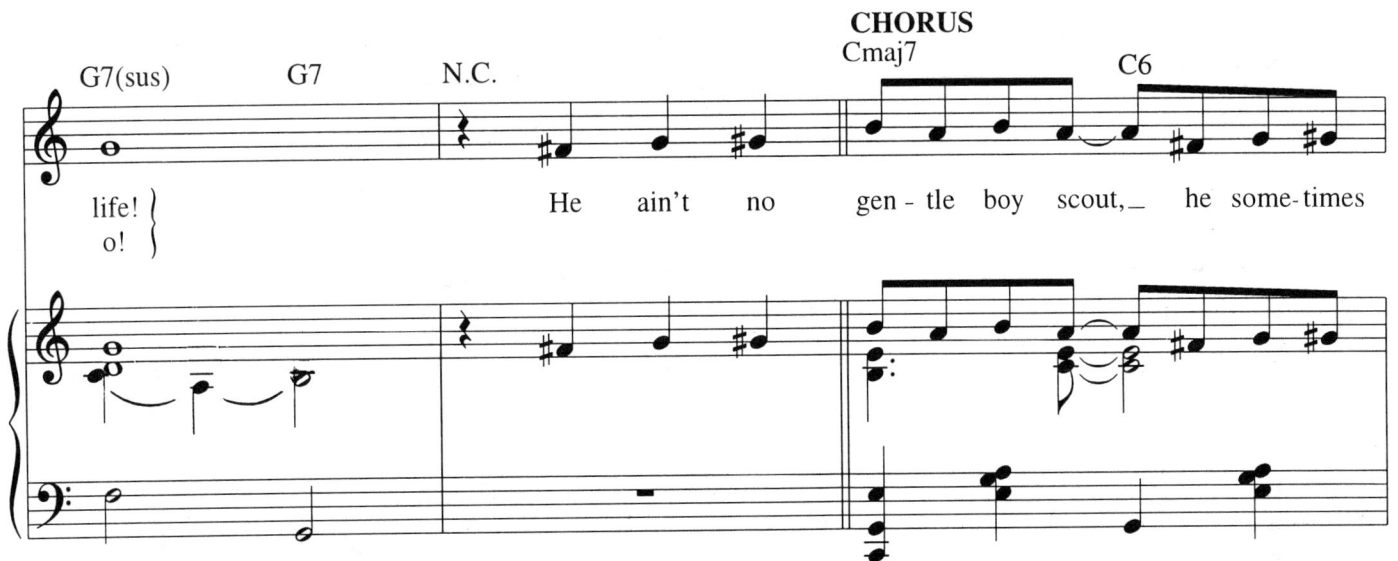

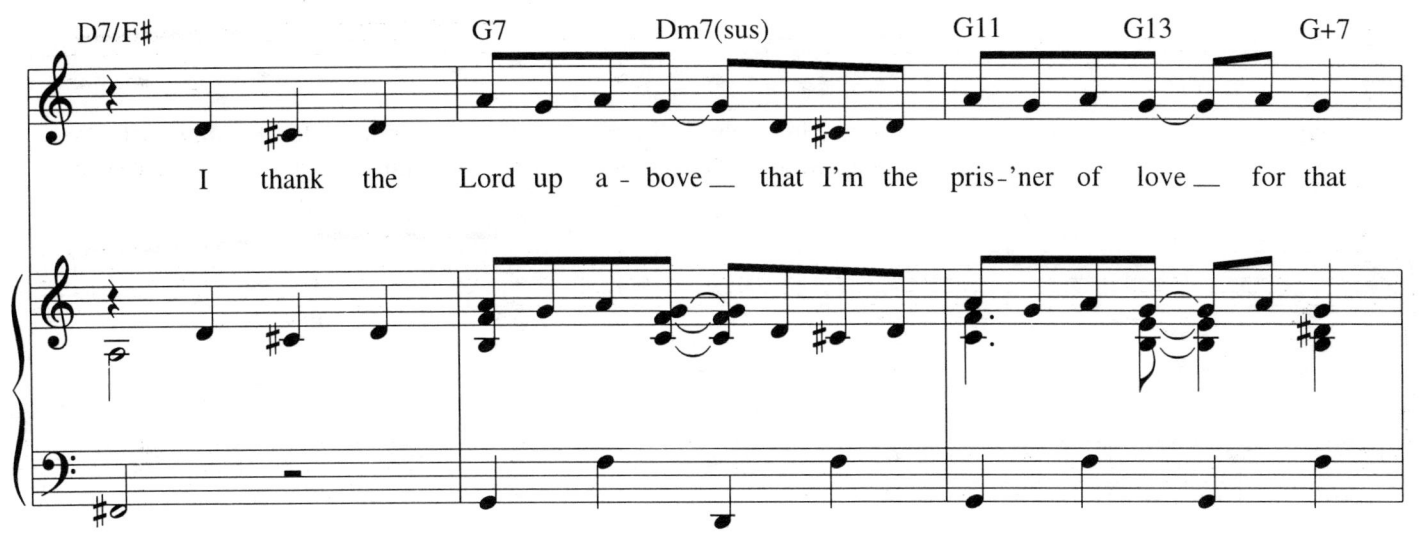

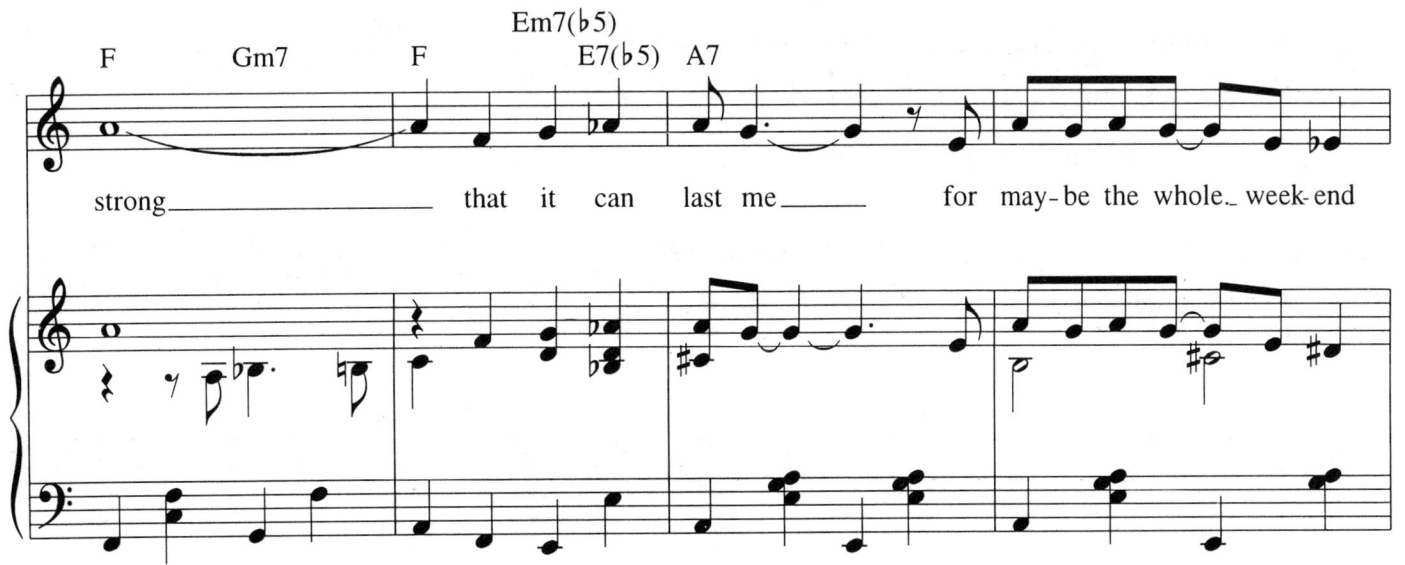

3. In the tradition of countless marines,
   Go Hollywood!
   Tuck your equipment in super-tight jeans,
   Go Hollywood.

Saunter the boulevard-You're out for hire
Milk all you can out of old men's desire
'Cause in just a few years you'll find that you are the buyer,
—That's Hollywood!

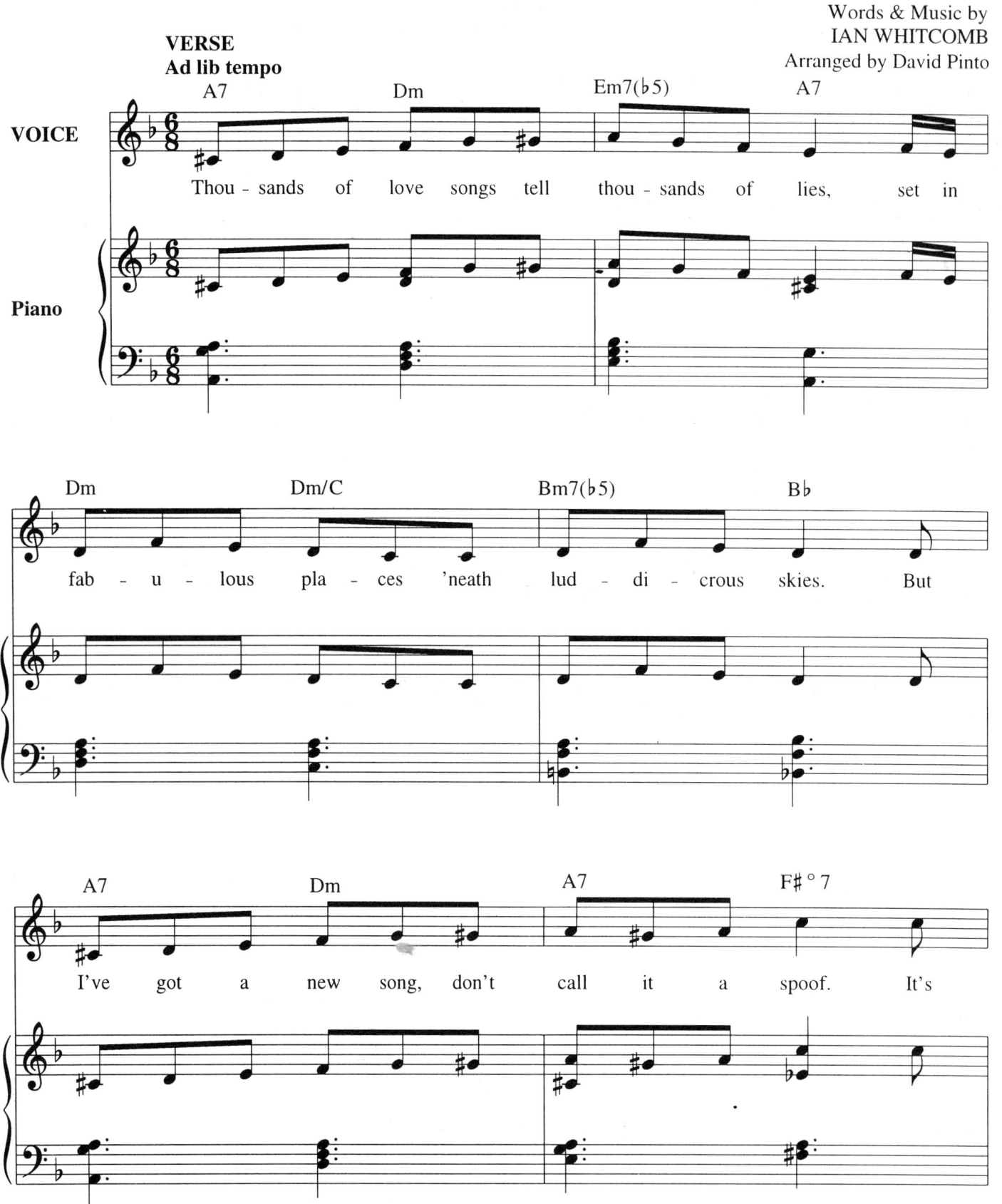

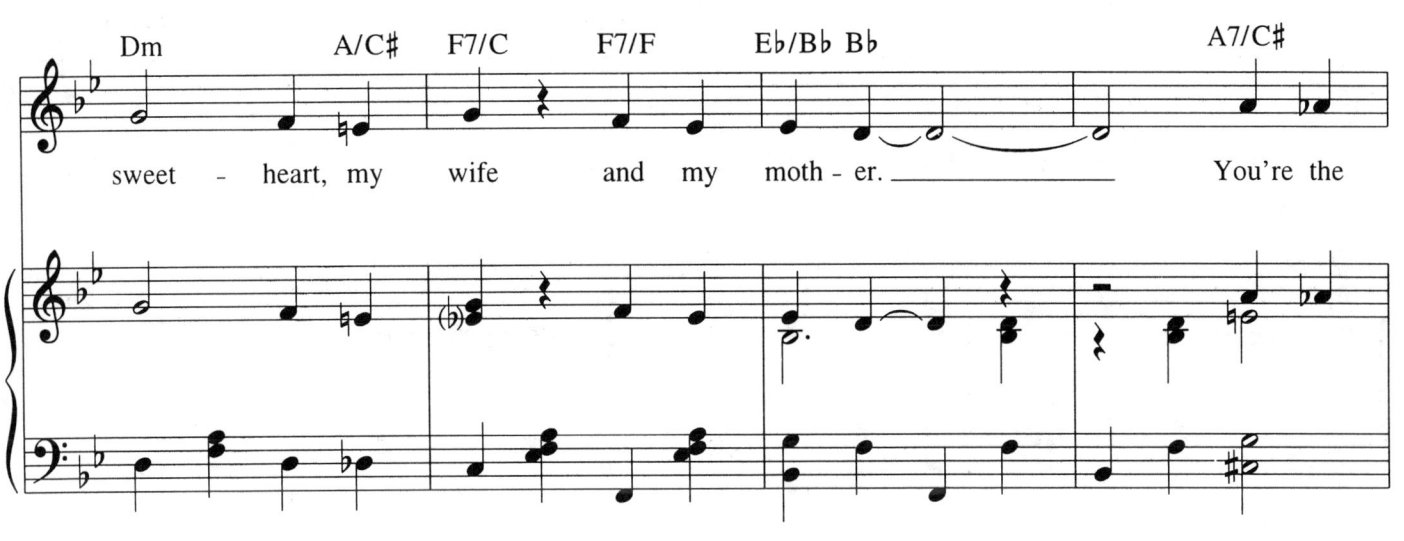

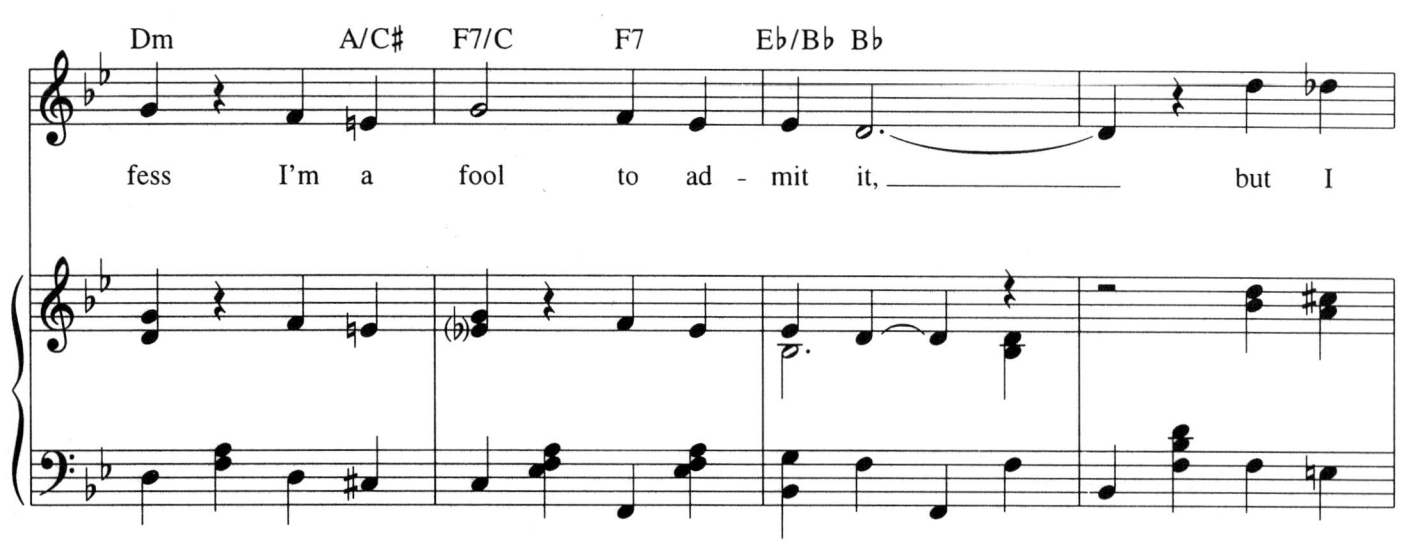

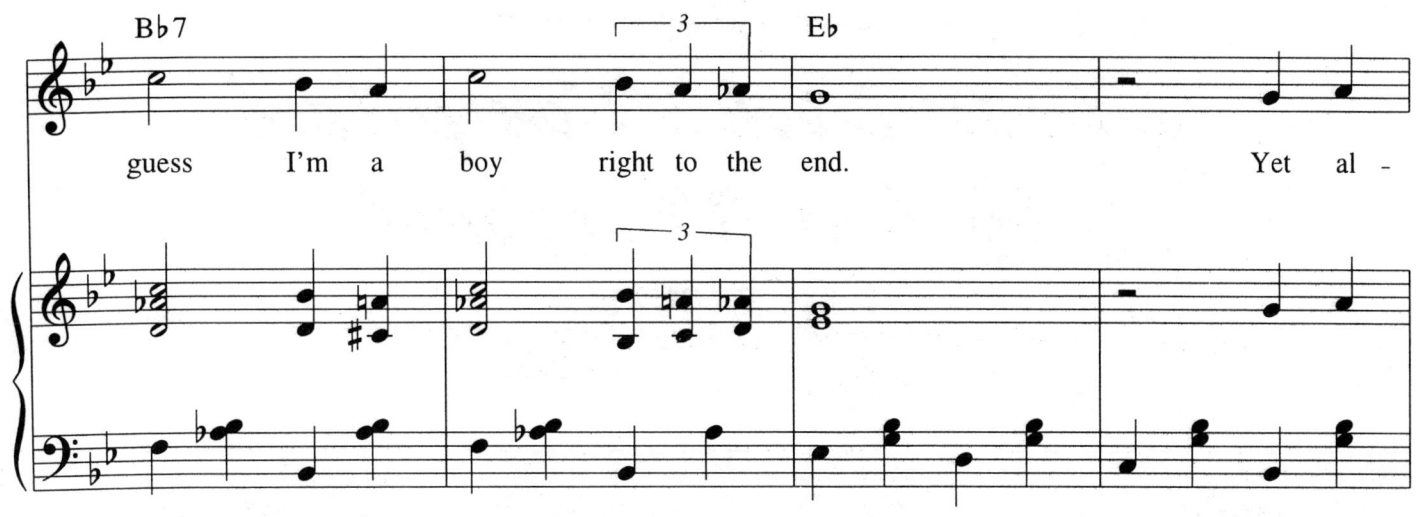

Other Books Compiled by Ian Whitcomb

Treasures of Tin Pan Alley
By Ian Whitcomb. A collection of songs from the golden age of Tin Pan Alley. Includes *The Honeysuckle and the Bee; Under the Bamboo Tree; Alexander's Ragtime Band; Peg O' My Heart;* and many more. In piano/vocal format with guitar chords. Flex binding. (95370, Book and Cassette)

Vaudeville Favorites
Compiled & written by Ian Whitcomb, edited by Ronny Schiff. A compilation of original song sheets and their spectacular covers from the Vaudeville era. Includes a "History of Vaudeville," detailed stories about the songs and their songwriters, plus vintage photos. Flex binding. (95367, Book and CD)

Songs of the Ragtime Era
By Ian Whitcomb. This celebration of the rowdy Ragtime Era is a fun romp through the sounds of American music from 1895 to 1918. Includes 28 songs, featuring original sheet music with covers, period photographs and background on each song and its composer. (96194BCD, Book/CD Set)

The Best of Vintage Dance
By Ian Whitcomb. This book provides a setting and a historical background from which to enter the wonderful world of vintage ballroom dancing. It contains a treasury of waltzes, two steps, one steps, fox trots, tangos, ragtime novelties and grand marches. (95496BCD, Book/CD Set)

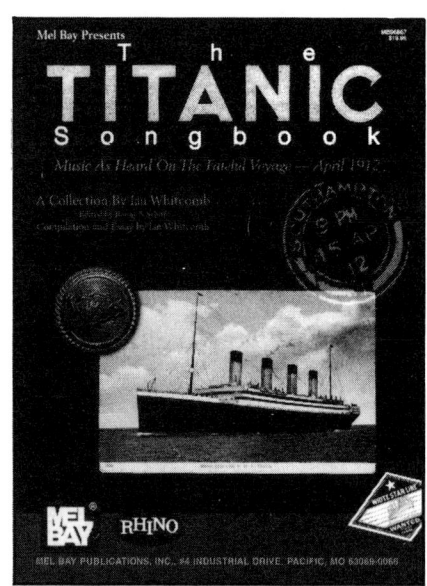

The Titanic Songbook
By Ian Whitcomb, edited by Ronny S. Schiff. Presents authentic period music, ranging from classical to ragtime, as performed on the fateful voyage of the *Titanic* on April 4, 1912. A full recording of the music perfomed by Ian and his White Star Orchestra is also available. (96867, Book and CD)

Titanic Tunes "Songs from Steerage"
By Ian Whitcomb. Following the success of *The Titanic Songbook,* Ian Whitcomb has compiled this collection of 20 Music Hall Songs. This book is a musical/historical tour of force. Features historical essays and anecdotes plus vintage photographs. Piano/vocal format. (98058, Book and CD)